ALSO BY JOHN SAGER

A Tiffany Monday – an Unusual Love Story, West Bow Press 2012

Joan's Gallery, 50 Years of Artistry by Joan Johnson Sager, Blurb, Inc. 2013

Uncovered – My Half-Century with the CIA, West Bow Press 2013

Night Flight, A Novel, Create Space, 2013

Operation Night Hawk, A Novel, Create Space, 2014

Moscow at Midnight, A Novel, Create Space, 2014

The Jihadists' Revenge, A Novel, Create Space, 2014

Mole, A Novel, Create Space, 2015

Capital Crises, A Novel, Create Space, 2015

God's Listeners, An Anthology, Create Space, 2015

Crescent Blood, A Novel, Create Space 2016

Sasha, from Stalin to Obama, A Biography, Create Space 2016

Shahnoza – Super Spy, A Novel, Create Space, 2016

Target Oahu, A Novel, Create Space, 2017

Aerosol, A Novel, Create Space, 2017

The Health Center, A Novel, Create Space, 2017

The Conservator, A Biography, Create Space, 2017

The Evil Alliance, A Novel, Create Space, 2018

Tehran Revisited, A Novel, Archway Publishers, 2019

St. Barnabas, A Novel, Inspiring Voices, 2019

The Caravan, A Novel, Outskirts Press, 2019

Senator McPherson, A Novel, Inspiring Voices, 2019

Meetings in Moscow, A Novel, Outskirts Press, 2019

Madam President, A Novel, Outskirts Press, 2019

Kiwi Country, A Novel, Outskirts Press, 2020

Conquering Covid, A Novel, Inspiring Voices, 2020

Coping With Covid, A Novel, Inspiring Voices, 2021

WUHAN REVISITED

A Novel

JOHN SAGER

authorHOUSE®

AuthorHouse™
1663 Liberty Drive
Bloomington, IN 47403
www.authorhouse.com
Phone: 833-262-8899

Published by AuthorHouse 04/15/2021

ISBN: 978-1-6655-2305-9 (sc)
ISBN: 978-1-6655-2303-5 (hc)
ISBN: 978-1-6655-2304-2 (e)

Library of Congress Control Number: 2021908175

If I go and prepare a place for you, I will come again and receive you to Myself, that where I am, there you may be also.

John 14:3

CONTENTS

AUTHOR'S NOTE

Although this is a work of fiction, the reader might wish to be informed of the ongoing controversy regarding the origins of the Novel Coronavirus—in Wuhan—and its deadly offspring, Covid-19.

The Wuhan lab at the core of a virus controversy

by Jing Xuan Teng With Laurie Chen In Beijing

Nestled in the hilly outskirts of Wuhan, the city at the heart of the coronavirus crisis, a Chinese high-security biosafety laboratory is now the subject of US claims it may be the cradle of the pandemic.

Chinese scientists have said the virus likely jumped from an animal to humans in a market that sold wildlife in Wuhan, but the existence of the lab has fueled conspiracy theories that the germ spread from the facility.

The United States has now brought the allegations into the mainstream, with Secretary of State Mike Pompeo saying US officials are doing a "full investigation" into how the virus "got out into the world".

Here are some key questions about the Wuhan Institute of Virology (WIV):

What is it?

The institute is home to the China Centre for Virus Culture Collection, the largest virus bank in Asia which preserves more than 1,500 strains, according to its website.

The complex contains Asia's first maximum security lab equipped to handle Class 4 pathogens (P4)—dangerous viruses that pose a high risk of person-to-person transmission, such as Ebola.

The 300-million-yuan ($42 million) lab was completed in 2015, and finally opened in 2018, with the founder of a French bio industrial firm, Alain Merieux, acting as a consultant in its construction.

The institute also has a P3 laboratory that has been in operation since 2012.

The 3,000-square-metre (32,000-square-foot) P4 lab, located in a square building with a cylindrical annex, lies near a pond at the foot of a forested hill in Wuhan's remote outskirts.

On a recent visit, AFP saw no sign of activity inside.

A poster outside the complex read, "Strong Prevention and Control, Don't Panic, Listen to Official Announcements, Believe in Science, Don't Spread Rumors".

Is it the source of the coronavirus?

Pompeo said Friday that Chinese authorities themselves, when they started investigating the virus, "considered whether the WIV was, in fact, the place where this came from".

"We know they've not permitted the world's scientists to go into that laboratory to evaluate what took place there, what's happening there, what's happening there even as we speak," he said in a radio interview.

US diplomatic cables seen by The Washington Post revealed that officials were especially concerned about inadequate safety standards related to researchers' handling of SARS-like bat coronaviruses in the high-security lab.

Fox News said the pandemic's "patient zero" may have been

infected by a strain of bat virus being studied at the facility that somehow got into the population in Wuhan.

Various conspiracy theories about the alleged origin of the coronavirus in the lab have flourished online.

The institute declined to comment on Friday, but it released a statement in February dismissing the rumors.

It said it received samples of the then-unknown virus on December 30, determined the viral genome sequence on January 2 and submitted information on the pathogen to the World Health Organization on January 11.

Chinese foreign ministry spokesman Zhao Lijian on Friday rejected allegations that the lab was responsible for the outbreak.

"A discerning person will understand at a glance that the purpose is to create confusion, divert public attention, and shirk their responsibility," said Zhao, who himself promoted conspiracy theories the US army may have brought the virus to China.

What do scientists know about the virus?

Scientists believe the virus originated in bats before being passed to humans through an intermediary species—possibly the endangered pangolin, whose scales are illegally trafficked in China for traditional medicine.

But a study by a group of Chinese scientists published in *The Lancet* in January revealed that the first COVID-19 patient had no connection to Wuhan's infamous animal market, and neither did 13 of the first 41 confirmed cases.

Institute researcher Shi Zhengli, one of China's leading experts on bat coronaviruses and the deputy director of the P4 lab, was part of the team that published the first study to suggest that SARS-CoV-2 came from bats.

In an interview with Scientific American, Shi said the SARS-CoV-2 genome sequence did not match any of the bat coronaviruses her laboratory had previously collected and studied.

Filippa Lentzos, biosecurity researcher at King's College London, said while there is currently no proof for the lab accident theory, there is also "no real evidence" that the virus came from the wet market.

"For me, the pandemic origin is still an open question," Lentzos told AFP.

There are some indications "that could point to a potential lab accident from basic scientific research", she said.

"But all of this needs considerable investigation for anyone to say anything with any certainty on the pandemic origins."

David Heymann, professor of infectious disease epidemiology at the London School of Hygiene and Tropical Medicine, also said there was no evidence about its origin but it is "closely related to a bat virus".

"There are many theories of how humans could've been infected, and I don't think any of them are able to be substantiated at present."

ONE

*T*hursday afternoon in Washington, DC's district courthouse, judge Timothy Watkins presiding. Attorney Jeffry Winslow is presenting his wrap-up statement to the jury. The trial is in its third day and the prosecuting attorney—veteran William Meyer—has been able to produce only two witnesses, neither of which was as credible as he would have liked.

"Ladies and gentlemen, you've now heard all the evidence. The prosecution has attempted to prove that my client, Jonas Hammond, committed that robbery of Washington's Riggs Bank, a theft of some eighty thousand dollars, in cash. As you know, bank robbery is a serious offence, punishable by up to twenty years in prison. The fact that Mr. Hammond is a black man has not been mentioned, but we all know that his being black is something the prosecution hopes will influence your decision. You know, too, that for many years our court rooms,

1

everywhere, are expected to be color-blind. And when you gather in the jury room you should keep this in mind.

"You should also remember the testimony of Mary Anne Jensen, she also a person of color. Miss Jensen, under oath, has sworn that the man who took that money is *not* Mr. Hammond. As the teller from whom the money was taken, she certainly should know.

"Of course, the prosecution has attempted to refute Miss Jensen's testimony by claiming she can't be certain because whoever *did* take the money was wearing a mask. Our response to that assertion is that these days *everyone* is wearing a mask.

"Now then, in a few minutes judge Watkins will give the twelve of you instructions on how you are to consider the evidence. Tomorrow is Friday and if you are able to reach a verdict before the end of the day you won't have to be sequestered over the weekend. And, although it shouldn't matter, the weather forecast calls for a heavy snowfall, beginning about midnight.

"And I wish you well."

After less than two hours of deliberation, the jury found for the defense. Jonas Hammond was declared innocent and has returned to his home in Bethesda, Maryland.

The next morning, a Saturday, four of the five attorneys of the Washington, DC law firm Smithers, Jensen, Hardy and Winslow are seated around the firm's conference table.

"Thank God the snowplows are working; even so, it took me almost an hour to get here. Had to stop at an Esso station to get some help with the chains.

"Well, Jeffry, what do you think? Was that a slam dunk or not?"

"Jim, these trials are never easy. Fortunately, we had an eye witness to the robbery and her testimony is what won the case for us. But now that everybody knows what happened—three TV channels and five radio stations—the police are trying to find the person who *did* rob that bank. We all know he was a black man but that's not going to help very much. My guess is that with all the publicity out there, whoever did this will be lying low for a very long time."

Two men, Richard (Dickey) Hudson and his friend Toby Adams, are seated in a booth in Bethesda's Townhall Tavern. Adams is on a one-month furlough from the Bethesda County jail, the presiding judge having agreed to the arrangement but only after his attorney has posted a one thousand dollar bond.

Hudson has been in and out of several Maryland correctional institutions, always for either buying or selling small packages of diluted cocaine. At the moment he is clean and able to function.

Toby is the first to speak.

"Well, Dickey, you sure got away with one. Whatcha gonna do with all that money?"

"Right now it's in the trunk of my car, 820 one hundred dollar bills."

"Eighty two thousand bucks, all in cash!?"

"That's right, Friend. And I can deposit it—a few hundred at time—right here in Bethesda's First National bank. My brother Ted has an account there and he knows what's going on."

"Does he know how much dough we're talking about?"

"Not yet, but I promised him ten percent of whatever the loot amounts to. Hell, he'll be the happiest guy in town!"

"When will this happen?"

"He'll go to his bank first thing in the morning, I think it opens at ten."

Unbeknownst to Richard Hudson, every bank in the Washington, DC area was put on notice. A computerized printout of the serial number of each stolen bill was sent by email, to appear on the computer screens of those banks. Teller Margaret Fisher has asked for an appointment with her bank's manager.

"Excuse me, Mr. Rogers, but I've just run across something you should know."

"Sure, Marge, what is it?"

"You remember that robbery, a few weeks ago?"

"Of course, it made headlines."

"Well, Sir, one of those stolen bills just came across my computer screen. And I have the signature of the man who wanted to add it to his account. A man by the name of Theodore Hudson. He's had an account her for several years and as far as I know has never been in trouble.

"But the application for his account lists a brother, Richard Hudson. The Hudson family is black, and that may account for something."

"Thank you, Marge. I'm afraid this is above my pay grade, yours, too. I'm going to notify Sergeant Richard Hardy. He's part of Bethesda's Criminal Investigations division. I'm sure he can take it from there."

The next morning

"Hey, Sarge, here's an email from a Larry Rogers, he's the manager of Washington's Riggs bank."

"Yeah, I have the same thing on my computer. What do you make of it?

"Two plus two makes four, right? I'm thinking we have an ID on the guy who robbed that bank. But you'll need a warrant, if you intend to talk to him."

"Sure, that's routine. Judge Simmons will give me one on my say-so."

The interrogation lasted no more than two hours. Richard Hudson admitted to having most of the money still hidden in the trunk of his car. He pled guilty, to avoid a longer sentence. After a lengthy hearing before Judge Arnold Simmons—during which he waived his right of appeal—Hudson was sentenced to ten months in Bethesda's First Precinct jail.

<hr>

Friday afternoon at the Bethesda Manor nursing home. Eighty year old Harry Winslow and his wife Alice, each in a wheelchair, are seated near the activity room's fireplace.

"Well, Alice, I'd say our boy did pretty well. We saw his picture in the local news section of the *Bethesda Gazette* and a there was a 30-second video clip and channels five and seven."

"Yes, Sweetheart, and we can be so proud of him! You remember, of course, that when he graduated from Walt Whitman high school he wasn't sure what he wanted to do next. We both encouraged him to go to Georgetown University law school but he was afraid he'd be made fun of, as the son of a successful lawyer—you."

"True. And many people don't know the meaning of the

word *nepotism*, getting special treatment because of one's family connections. So both Jeffry and I had to think about that when I invited him to become part of my law firm.

"But he finished law school with a 3.2 gpa, and the bar exam was tough but he passed on his first try. So signing on as an intern made a lot of sense."

TWO

*S*ome background here. While Jeffry Winslow was attending Georgetown U's law school, he frequently visited the school's cafeteria which, at certain hours, was a quiet place, good for catch-up studying. On one of those occasions:

"Well, hello there! I don't believe I've seen you before."

"Probably not, I'm new here, and this is the first time I've been able to get away from my studies."

"And you are - - -?"

"Yes, I'm Chen Bu Ying, I'm a Chinese exchange student."

"Hmm, and you're English is nearly perfect! How come?"

"It's a long story but I can be brief. Some years ago, my father was appointed to become one of our representatives to the United Nations, in New York. He's been a diplomat for most of his adult life, speaks pretty good English, some French and, of course, our native Mandarin."

"By the way, it's okay for you to remove that mask you're wearing. You'll notice the tables are far enough apart to meet the school's social distancing requirements. And I'll do the same.

"Not to be nosy, but that makes you a Communist?"

"Of course. The Communists have been in power in Beijing ever since the days of Mao Tse-tung."

"Do people here know you're a Communist?"

"It hardly ever comes up. I'm not particularly proud of being a Communist but just about everybody at home is. Same for our diplomats, world wide."

"How did you like New York?"

"I hated it. Loud, smelly, no social life. Of course I was only a teen then and most of my friends were the children of other diplomats. But it was tough. Sure, I wanted to date but my parents were afraid I'd be raped. So I mostly stayed a home, with them—boring!"

"Hmm, yeah I can understand. You're a beautiful woman, Chen Bu, and I can see that even as a teen you'd be very appealing."

"Thank you Mr.- - -?"

"Winslow, Jeffry Winslow. But my friends call me Jeff and

you should too. But, again, not to be nosy, what are you doing here? You said you're an exchange student, but studying what?"

"No, Jeff, you're not being nosy, not at all. I'm doing graduate work in international relations. It's my father's influence, but it makes sense. Neither he nor I like the way our two countries are getting along and, we hope, some day we can make a difference."

"You say our two countries aren't getting along. Any ideas about why that is?"

"Sure, plenty. For one, even after two years, our leaders in Beijing are still denying that the Coronavirus pandemic got its start in that Wuhan lab. It's embarrassing. The whole world knows it's a lie.

"I have friends back home, one family lives in a suburb of Beijing, the other in Wuhan, where the Coronavirus got its start. They and most of their neighbors are afraid to speak out. They know how the propagandists work, one word spoken in the wrong place and the authorities want to know who said it and to whom. It's like it was in Moscow, when Joseph Stalin was in charge!"

"As we like to say, Chen Bu, you're on a role and I'm fascinated by every word. Tell me more. What was it like growing up, you said in a suburb of Beijing."

"I said my friends lived there; we were neighbors. One of their sons, twelve year old Li Wei, was a playmate of mine. In those days we kids didn't know much about Communism. Our teachers tired to teach us some of the movement's history but it wasn't interesting and hardly anyone paid attention.

"But even as children we knew that our parents, even grandparents, were careful not to say anything bad about the leaders in Beijing."

"What about your parents, Chen Bu, what was it like for them?"

"The entire Ying family was what you call dirt poor. My dad grew up in a village about fifty miles south of Beijing. He was orphaned at age six when his parents—my grandparents—were killed in a fire that destroyed nearly half their village. But some neighbors took him in and, eventually, he made it through those awful growing-up years and went to the University of Beijing's school of International Relations. He was a good student and, eventually, he was sent to New York City, as you now know."

"And your mother?"

"Yes, she was lucky, considering everything. She always wanted to be a ballet dancer but there were very few opportunities where she lived. When she was fifteen or so, one of those so-called talent scouts told her she would do very well but that she'd have to go to Moscow and join one of their ballet companies. He said she was beautiful enough that she'd be welcomed at first sight. But, of course, that was only a dream. No way could she have left China, the authorities wouldn't allow it. But she has thrived in New York. My father was obliged to host dinner parties for those diplomats at the United Nations and my mom had developed the reputation of being the perfect hostess, beautiful to look at, charming and an excellent dancer.

"But, you might be able to imagine what it was like, seeing those huge portraits of Mao and Stalin, on every building wall, even in the classrooms. I remember that someone wrote a song, the lyrics praised Mao and we kids were ordered to learn the words and then sing them at the beginning of each school day. It was just awful and I'll never forget it!"

"Uh, Chen Bu, I see it's about time to be getting back to class. I'd like very much to see more of you. There's a little restaurant across the street, *The Georgetown Gathering.* We could have dinner there, say about six. Would you go for that? The management requires its patrons to wear a mask but after we're seated we can take them off."

"Sure, Jeff. I'd love it."

THREE

A few words about Georgetown.

It's a charming area with Federal-style architecture, cobblestone streets and fashion and design shops. The dining scene is defined by upmarket restaurants and waterfront seafood spots, while nightlife spans boisterous college bars, traditional taverns and intimate live music lounges. Georgetown Waterfront Park has a riverside promenade and gardens, and there's a bike path along the C&O Canal. Owning—or renting—a Georgetown townhouse is expensive and time-consuming, as some of the structures are at least one hundred years old and require careful maintenance. Although the university of the same name is within walking distance, very few students can afford to live there. Those adults who do live there considered it a badge of honor. Residents include several congress persons, one Supreme Court judge and several very expensive attorneys.

Their meal together couldn't have been better. Rather than searching the menu for Chinese food, Chen Bu insisted on ordering something typically American. So they chose medium rare prime ribs, scalloped potatoes, asparagus tips in Bearnaise sauce, a ten year old California Merlot and, for dessert, champagne and Baklava. On the drive back to her apartment, Chen Bu thought that with all that alcohol in their bloodstreams the two of them might consider going to bed. But, she decided, best to save that for later. She knew she was falling in love with this oh-so-fascinating young man. And, for all she knew, he with her.

At her apartment door, Chen Bu asked Jeff to kiss her goodnight.

"Thanks so much, Jeff. We should see a lot more of each other."

"You can count on it Chen Bu. You need to know that for now, at least, you're the only woman in my life."

The next morning, early, Jeff showered, shaved, ate his usual breakfast of one banana and a bowl of Wheaties, V-8 juice and coffee. Then he walked into his apartment's small living room, plopped into his Lazy Boy chair and begin talking to himself.

"What have you got yourself into, Jeffry? One or two more get-togethers and the two of you are likely to want to go to bed. That should never happen and you know it. This is one beautiful woman and she's probably smarter than you. Eventually, she'll be going back to China. And even if the two of you decided to get married, there's no way you could go with her.

"You've never told her about your inheritance, the seventy-five million dollars your grandfather bequeathed you in his will. So far, *no one* knows about this, except you and your parents. Maybe some day you can share this with Chen Bu, but certainly not now.

"And, don't forget, her dad is a diplomat at the United Nations in New York; and I believe she said he'll be there for at least two more years. I wonder if she would consider betraying her county. She's said more than once that she doesn't think much of the regime in Beijing. Maybe I should get in touch with the FBI. Their headquarter is right here in Washington. Yeah, that's what I'll do."

<hr />

0930 hours, in the office of Special Agent Robert McPherson, FBI Washington Field Office. In response to Jeffry Winslow's telephone call, McPherson has invited him to meet in his conference room.

"So, Mr. Winslow, what's on your mind? You said it was important and that you think the FBI needs to know. Know what?"

"Yes, Sir. I'm about to - - -"

"You can call me Bob, like everybody else around here."

"Okay, Bob, here's the deal. I'm a graduate student at Georgetown U's law school. A week or so back, I met a Chinese woman in our school's cafeteria. Her name is Chen Bu Ying and she's studying international relations. Her father is a ranking diplomat in the Chinese delegation at the United Nations in New York."

"Pardon the interruption, but what has this to do with the FBI?"

"Yeah, I'm getting to that. Chen Bu has made it very clear that she doesn't think much of the Chinese Communist leaders in Beijing. As an example, she's embarrassed that her government still denies that it had anything to do with the Coronavirus outbreak in Wuhan. She says the whole world now knows this is a lie, a giant coverup, and she's very unhappy about this.

"When I asked her why she's studying international relations, she said it was her father's idea, that someday, they could help improve relations with the United States."

"What's your personal relationship with this woman?"

"Yeah, that's a huge problem. We love each other and would probably want to get married. Although, she probably thinks I'd never go back to China with her and she can't stay here much longer. Her visitor's visa expires next year.

"But here's where the rubber meets the road, in my opinion."

"Go!"

"I'm pretty sure that if it were done right, Chen Bu would agree to help the United States. She and her father talk to each other at least once each week. If the FBI could persuade her to become an informer, she could tell you all kinds of things."

"Jeff, what you're suggesting is that this woman betrays her country. If she's found out the Chines authorities would want her, dead or alive. Do you really believe she's willing to take that risk?"

"Yes, I do. But, remember, I said it has to be done right; that means very carefully, so that no one knows."

"Okay, Jeff. I want you to meet a woman, she's part of my staff. She's in her early 40s, speaks native Mandarin. Her name is Connie Woo, she came here when she was still a teen, cared for by her grandparents, part of the Chinatown community in San Francisco.

"Now, she has a top secret security clearance. I'll leave it to you to decide how to bring these two women together, but the sooner the better. Connie's an old pro, she's recruited several others and let's hope she can do the same with your Chen Bu.

"Of course that leads to the obvious question - - -"

"Which is?"

"How will you feel, arranging for you intended to become an informant for the FBI?"

"I can live with that. I'm sure she'll understand."

———◆———

The next morning, Jeff phones Chen Bu and asks her to meet him for coffee in the school's cafeteria.

"What's up, Sweetheart? You said you have something important to talk about."

"I do. You remember telling me you're studying international relations so that some day you might be able to help improve relations between our two countries?"

"Yes, of course. I'm quite serious about that."

"Okay. What I'm about to suggest may puzzle you, but I'm saying it with your future in mind, and mine, too, for that matter. If you *really* want to help you'll need my government's assistance. There's no way you and/or you and your father can change things without help."

"Yes, I suppose that makes sense. Where are you going with this?"

"Chen Bu, I know of a woman—her name is Connie Woo—like you she's Chinese. She's about 40, very mature, her relatives lived in San Francisco's Chinatown. She works for the FBI, right here in Washington- - -"

"What?!! The FBI?!"

"Yes, Sweetheart, the FBI. Like I said, if you really want to help you'll need my government's help *and* approval, and Connie Woo can make that possible, if you're willing to meet her."

"Well, okay, if you say so. How and when will this happen?"

"Connie has an office right here in Washington, in the FBI headquarters building. She'll be comfortable there and she'll explain what's involved. I don't believe the FBI uses the polygraph but they do have strict procedures to protect people like you and others who are helping them. You'll have to fill out some forms, background info about your past, that sort of thing and they'll run all that through their computers, just to make sure you've told the truth."

FOUR

*O*nce more, in the office of Special Agent Robert McPherson, FBI Washington Field Office. McPherson has decided he might as well have all his 'players' in his office at the same time. That way, there won't be any misunderstandings. McPherson is the first to speak.

"I'm glad you were able to come, on such short notice. I believe you've met each other while you were waiting outside. Jeff, you and I know each other well enough. Why don't you remind the others why we're here."

"Sure, Bob, glad to do that. Connie Woo, here, has become the key to what we're about. As you know by now, Connie is ethnic Chinese, speaks perfect English and Mandarin. She's had three meetings with Chen Bu and that's why Chen agreed to be here. I explained to Chen that at this meeting she would be told why she's here and what's expected of her."

"Yes, why *am* I here?!"

"Hmm, that's your cue, Bob. Tell us."

"Chen, you'll surely remember the forms you filled out yesterday. The good news is that we've run all that info through our computers and you're now cleared for Top Secret, something that almost never happens with a Chinese citizen."

"Why all the fuss?"

"Because we're going to ask you to provide us with information that we can't get anywhere else. And that begins with your father at the United Nations."

"Oh, my! Why?"

"We know that you and your father are quite close, you're on your smartphone with him at least once each day. We assume your father is a loyal Chinese diplomat but, probably, one with reservations about how his superiors in Beijing are dealing with the United States.

"You can tell us about that. And you shouldn't think you're betraying him or anyone else. What you tell us goes absolutely no farther. We turn your info into classified reports. Your name *never* appears in those reports. We assign you a pseudonym and that name stays with you for as long as you wish.

"For example, you can use your tablet and write out a summary of your most recent conversation with your father. You upload that summary to my office. It will be encoded and we'll show you how to do that. Same the other way, except that we'll always use our smartphone to contact you. Those voice messages are always encoded, and your response the same. So, it's perfectly secure.

"Now, I understand that you and Jeff Winslow have talked about getting married- - -"

"How do you know that? Shame on you!"

"Sorry to upset you Chen Bu, but we know a lot of things about a lot of people. That's one of the things we get paid for. But to be perfectly honest, we had considered asking you to go back to China, preferably to Wuhan where we know you have friends. But once you agree to something like that, we no longer would have jurisdiction. You may not know it, but the FBI's jurisdiction ends at the water's edge. Anything having to do with overseas activity belongs to the Central Intelligence Agency, the CIA."

"Yes, I've heard of them."

FIVE

*I*n the office of Herbert Jameson, chief of CIA's Far East division, China branch. Jameson is speaking to his deputy, Frances Meyer.

"What do you think, Fran?"

"Just what we've been hoping for, Herb. A young Chinese-American woman who wants to help. And as I understand it, she has friends in Wuhan."

"Yes, the Bureau already has agreed to turn her over to us, along with her husband, what's his name, Jeff Winslow?"

"Well, assuming she agrees to return to Wuhan, he'll want to go with her and, as far as we know, he doesn't speak a word of Mandarin."

"Hmm, you know, Fran, this is something I need to discuss with my friend over at State, Timothy Baxter. Tim has moved up the ladder and now is in charge of State's Cultural Affairs program, world-wide. As you know, we have a consulate in Wuhan and I'm thinking Tim would be willing to integrate Mr. Winslow into the Wuhan staff, say, as the number two cultural affairs officer. State has a special program for teaching its officers to speak Mandarin. I'm told that after three or four months of intensive study and practice, their students can speak Mandarin reasonably well."

"Yes, you're right. Once the two of them are settled in Wuhan, they can become a team, each one on his/her own moving about the area, talking to people and reporting back"

"Yes, and speaking of reporting, we understand the Bureau has already equipped them with modified iPhones and Apple tablets so they can report whatever they wish—via our embassy in Beijing, of course—and it's all perfectly secure, using one of our earth satellites."

"Okay. So what happens next?"

The process took six months to complete and for Jeff Winslow, the hurry-up-and-get-it-done crash course in the Mandarin language was the toughest thing he'd ever done. But, finally, his Chinese-American teacher told him he was good to go.

Next step, another crash course at the State Department's Bureau of Cultural Affairs. The program, approved by Secretary of State Raymond Larsen, taught Jeff more than he needed to know about the duties of a cultural affairs officer, the job he would have at the U.S. Consulate-General in Wuhan. To make his cover as believable as possible, he was given the rank of an FSR-4 (Foreign Service Reserve Officer); that pays him about $58,000 a year, somewhat less than he was making before.

It was no secret that career State Department officers resented the integration of CIA officials and at times the department flat-out refused the process, as was the case in the early days of the Cold War in Moscow. But United States president Owen Oglethorpe had made it clear that *he* approved the process and that put an end to the dispute.

SIX

W ord came down through the State Department's bureaucracy that Jeff Winslow and his wife were to be treated just like all the other overseas-bound personnel. That meant a visit with the department's medical staff where they were inoculated against typhus, typhoid fever, smallpox and diphtheria.

Then, the first of two injections of the Pfizer Covid 19 vaccination and two weeks later the second. Then they were tested for the presence of the coronavirus pathogen and, when that test showed they were pathogen-free they were issued the Kitsbow Wake Protech Reusable Face Mask, believed to be the best protection currently available.

"You can wear these on the plane, as soon as you depart San Francisco. You may remove them IF the flight attendants say it's okay to do so, but before you get off the plane in Shanghai, put them on and keep them on until you believe it is safe to remove them. Use your own best judgment and good luck!"

———◆———

The nonstop flight from Dulles International to San Francisco was uneventful, the Delta Boeing 767 taking a little under five hours. Once inside the transit lounge at San Francisco's International airport, the travelers discovered that everyone was wearing a mask, passengers, baggage handlers, flight crews, even the janitors. There were several security officials, meandering about, but clearly intent on making sure that everyone was wearing a mask.

"What do you think, Chen Bu. We'll be here for two hours before our flight leaves for Shanghai. There's a small restaurant over there, we can do lunch, take a nap and we'll be ready."

The restaurant's menu was printed in both English and Chinese, clearly a recognition of the large Chinese-American community in the city's Chinatown. Ordering lunch was easy:

two bowls of Wonton soup, egg rolls, steamed seaweed, hot tea and, of course, the Chinese 'fortune cookies.'

Chen Bu couldn't resist a huge grin as she read hers: 'You are about to enter a new chapter in your life.' Jeff's read: 'Whatever it is, get used to it."

Their suite at Shanghai's Park View hotel was just as the brochures had advertised, more than comfortable with 24/7 room service. Jeff knew that the State Department's travel orders would never cover such an extravagant expense and he decided to tell Chen Bu about his inheritance, seventy-five million dollars. It made sense because, eventually, he' be paying for the Wuhan homeless shelter, part of the plan that had been agreed to before they left Washington.

"You what?! My God, Jeff, why didn't you tell me this before?"

"Because very few people know about this, Sweetheart, It's almost unheard of that a private citizen—me—would be allowed to do something like this. And we agreed, before leaving Washington, that the fewer people who know, the better. My new boss, Dick Albright—he's the Consul General in Wuhan—he knows, and so does our ambassador in our embassy in Beijing, Franklin Hatfield."

"Well, okay, if you say so. But never in my wildest dreams did I ever expect to be married to a man who's worth that much!"

"As they say Chen Bu, not to worry. Let's go down to this fabulous restaurant we've heard so much about, have dinner and get a good night's rest. We'll be flying to Wuhan tomorrow morning and I think it's safe to say that once we arrive and get settled, our lives will never be the same."

SEVEN

Before leaving Washington, Jeff made reservations for the flight from Shanghai to Wuhan, Chinese Eastern Airlines, two hours nonstop. The couple was pleased to learn that the aircraft was a Boeing 727 but as they left the boarding area they were reminded that each passenger was required to wear a mask and that only 75 passengers would be allowed to board, this to meet the social distancing requirements, still in place.

Inflight service was limited to hot tea and a chicken salad sandwich, no alcohol. Just as well, Jeff thought. He was about to meet his new boss and he wanted to be alert.

Richard Albright, with the rank of FSO-1, was on the State Department's short list of career Foreign Services officers who had qualified for the position of ambassador, requiring only a presidential appointment and a sign-off from the Senate's Foreign Relations committee. Fluent in French and Mandarin, the Wuhan Consulate General slot was his stepping stone to an ambassadorship, probably to the embassy in Beijing or, less likely, to Paris.

One of the department's brightest stars, Albright and his wife Suzanne had moved up the ladder faster than most, and Suzanne had much to do with that.

Her maiden name was Wang Lee Ying—whose meaning is *beautiful*—one of those rare cases wherein the name fits its owner. The daughter of a prosperous Chinese businessman, at age seventeen she was sent to San Francisco's Chinatown, there to learn to speak American English and learn American ways. Her father had reminded her that the United States and China had become the world's leading economies and it was vital that the competition remain intense but friendly and not threatening to other nations. And, he insisted, if she could help make that happen, it would become her highest calling.

Within weeks of arriving on post at Wuhan, Wang Lee set about to make her new home—the United States Consulate General in Wuhan—a place where everyone was welcome: foreign diplomats, Chinese officials, local merchants and, especially, Chinese citizens of every stripe: peasants, factory workers, merchants, school teachers everyone.

Albright had gone to the Foreign Service foreign language school at Monterrey, California and after one year of intensive study and practice, he could speak Mandarin nearly as well as his wife. Soon after the couple's arrival in Wuhan, Wang Lee let it be known that Saturday evenings would be reserved for entertaining in the consulate building's small ballroom. She hired a five-piece orchestra, contracted with a local print shop for engraved invitations and composed a list of invitees.

Among these: Wang Zhonglin, Wuhan's top Communist Party leader, a man beholden only to his rulers in Beijing. Wang thought of himself as the ruler of Wuhan—even all of Hubei province—every important decision affecting the region's population had to have his approval. If Wang Lee's invitation was accepted, the other guests would be honored to have their names included alongside the region's most important—and feared— political figure.

Then there was Dr. Li Jun Fang, the region's leading epidemiologist and the man who still insists that the Coronavirus did *not* originate in his Wuhan laboratory. There is some risk here, of course, because Wang Lee knows that should the good doctor accept her invitation, he likely will be accosted by the other guests as the man ultimately responsible for the massive disinformation campaign that Beijing's leaders have authorized.

Also, Li Min Woo, the forty-something director of Hubei province's opera company. Still a beautiful woman, Li Min's contralto voice was something to behold. She no longer performed on-stage, but her many recordings were among the hottest sellers in China's DVD market. Her husband, Wang Yong Woo, owned and operated Wuhan's largest shopping mall, making him one of the wealthiest men in the province.

To add some diversity to her list, she consulted the office directory and found Li Jie Won, the manager-director of Wuhan's largest grocery chain, something akin to the Kroger corporation at home, providing all manner of foodstuffs for some fifty million people. Won's wife, Li Min Won, was an established fashion designer and even at age forty-two, one of the most beautiful women in the province.

Last but not least, Wang Yong Jun, age 24, single, the consulate's trustworthy gofer. Unfortunately for Wang Lee Ying, she was unaware that Wang Yong had been suborned by the Chinese Ministry of State Security and was reporting, regularly, on the goings and comings of every American diplomat assigned to Hubei province. Because the young man had his own private quarters within the consulate's compound, he was free to come and go as he pleased, but always with a report for his MSS handler.

EIGHT

Wuhan's airport was the central air transit hub for all of Hubei province. Prior to the pandemic its influx of tourists had numbered in the hundreds each day, most American tourists but also a mix of European visitors, especially those who could speak either Mandarin or English. Many of them were booked on Viking River Cruises' *Century Sky,* a two-hundred-passenger river craft that plied the Yangtze River three times a week. Its passengers, most of them, were awed as they passed through the enormous locks of the Three Gorges dam, the largest hydroelectric project on Planet Earth. Unfortunately for thousands of Chinese residents—many of them peasants— the river would eventually flood their modest homes, farms and shops. Local activists complained bitterly with the rulers in Beijing, but to no avail.

Jeff and Chen Bu had seen photographs of Richard Albright, so it was easy enough to find him waiting in the transit area of Wuhan's international airport. He was accompanied by a young Chinese man, identified as the consulate's do-everything helper, name of Li Jun Wong.

"So good to see you two, finally, after waiting much too long. Welcome to Wuhan!!"

"Thank you, Sir, we're happy to be here. Yes, it has been a long time. My wife, Chen Bu here, tells me my Mandarin is good enough to get by and I expect it will improve with time."

"Let's forget the Sir stuff, Jeff. My friends call me Richard and you should, too. We need to move on to baggage claim and then we'll be on our way. It's about a half-hour drive to our offices, depending on traffic. The local authorities banned rickshaws about ten years ago, so it's mostly trucks and cars; no EVs yet, thank the Good Lord. As soon as we're out of the terminal you can remove your masks.

"Li Jun has his own car and he'll take your luggage directly to your quarters. He's been with us for five years now and is completely trustworthy.

"How about eating? When was your last meal?"

"Not a problem, Richard, we had dinner on the flight, about an hour ago. By the way, and before I forget, Larry Dawson asked to be remembered to you. As you probably know, he was recently promoted to head up State's foreign language program. He spent hours patiently listening to me struggle with Mandarin. I was surprised at how well he speaks it."

"Yes, I know. Larry married a Chinese-American woman who grew up in San Francisco's Chinatown. He tells me it's a perfect match; she wants a couples of kids, he's not so sure. But, as you saw, his Mandarin is good enough for him to run the school.

"I assume you're up to date on our project. The Department was reluctant at first, but when I assured them you'd be paying for most of it, they agreed to go ahead."

"Yeah, they told me in Washington that this would be the first time, ever, that a private citizen has agreed to fund a homeless shelter, anywhere. But we can afford it and we're anxious to get going. We understand there's a small hotel within walking distance of the consulate and we're prepared to buy the place and that will be our shelter."

"Yes, the owners have agreed to sell but they understand that their staff will say on. Two cooks, two housekeepers, three dining room servers, even a janitor. It's a ten-story building with 170 apartments. So at minimum, there's good living space for 170 homeless folks. Many more for those who are married."

"Parking?"

"Limited, and only for employees. We expect those who are still living in cars will be the first to move in. There's already a waiting list, last time I checked it was up to about fifty."

"What about liability insurance? The local authorities know about this, will they object?"

"Doesn't matter. We'll have a blanket policy written by MetLife, keep the Chinese out of it. And that policy, by the way, includes health insurance, for every homeless person who moves in."

"Covid?"

"Yeah, that's still a problem, sad to say. It's been pretty well stamped out but now and then someone will come down with it. There may be something like herd immunity going on here, what with just about every resident either having had Covid-19 or been exposed to it. We should be more concerned about tuberculosis, typhoid and smallpox. So far as I know, there's no way to be immune to those killers."

———◆◆◆———

The drive to the consulate compound took about 35 minutes. Lin Jun proved to be a very good driver, dodging in and out of the city's every which way traffic. As he slowed to a stop, an armed U.S Marine staff sergeant stood in front of the wrought iron gate and when he recognized the passengers he saluted, pushed a button and the gate opened. Once inside, the new arrivals felt like they were almost home again. They could see three United States flags fluttering in the breeze; the directional signs were in both English and Mandarin, the sloping lawns and gardens had recently been trimmed, and a display of pink heather lined the driveway.

"That's where you'll be staying," Lin Jun in his nearly perfect English. " Your housekeeper is Zhang Li Woo. She's very good at what she does, she's been with us for the past ten years. I'd guess she's about 30, still single, no boyfriends that I'm aware of. She can cook, sew, wash and iron your clothes; she even plays the piano, IF you ask her to when she's in the mood. And her English is nearly perfect, although she'd prefer that you use your Mandarin when speaking with her.

"A few more words about your quarters. It's a three-bedroom, two story building. Kitchen, dining room, laundry and toilet facilities on the ground floor. Upstairs, the three bedrooms, a sitting room, two bathrooms and an electric fireplace. In the basement you'll find a walk-in freezer, gas-fired furnace, a three-ton air conditioner and a small workbench.

"I understand you'll be doing some entertaining and this is where you'll do it. There's a pre-wired intercom system and all you do to activate is use your iPhone, tap the send icon and everything should work. There are voice-activated speakers throughout the building so you can speak and be heard any time you wish."

"Wow! Thanks for info, Lin Jun. You've covered everything I can think of. How about you, Chen Bu?"

"Marvelous, Sweetheart. But, truth be told, after all that travel, I'm tired. It's getting dark so perhaps we can have a snack and then go to bed?"

"Good idea. Let's do it!"

NINE

Zhang Li lived up to her reputation. When Jeff and Chen Bu walked into the dining room, they saw the table adorned with a display of red, white and blue flowers and a hand-written drawing with the words WELCOME! Inscribed on its surface. As soon as the couple was seated, Zhang Li appeared.

"I believe you know who I am, I'm your do-everything helper. Unfortunately, we don't have any American newspapers but we do have the Hubei Province *This Morning*. It's a kind of regional newspaper: current events, entertainment, comics, even an obituary column. This morning's issue's front page is all about the current World Health Organization's investigation of the origins of the coronavirus, a very contentious issue, as you might imagine. One of the paper's editorialists claims that your State Department isn't satisfied with the official explanation of what happened in that laboratory. I mention this only because you two, as Americans, can expect to be asked some hard questions."

"Thanks, Zhang Li. Yes, you're right. But we're prepared."

"Good. What can I get you from our kitchen? Anything American is okay."

"Chen Bu is a light eater. Tea and a bowl of cereal would be fine."

"And you?"

"Okay. Two slices of wheat toast with butter and strawberry jam, two poached eggs and two strips of bacon. I'd prefer coffee to tea, if you have it."

"Not a problem. Give me ten minutes."

After breakfast, the couple walked the short distance to the consular building's offices. Jeff had insisted that Chen Bu be with him, as they were about to meet Jeff's new boss, Richard Albright, and he wanted his wife to be there.

Somewhat to their surprise, a different Marine guard was at the welcome desk, just inside the building's entrance.

"I'm gunnery sergeant Michael Olsen, Sir. I'm in charge of

the Marine Corps security detachment here. There are five us and we're on duty here 24/7. You and your wife don't need a visitor's badge because we know you're here permanently. Mr. Albright is expecting you, his office is one flight up, first door on your right. Fortunately, the elevator is working today. We rely on the local Chinese engineers to keep it working but sometimes they mess up."

"Thanks, Sergeant, we'll remember that."

In Albright's office - - -

"What we're about to talk about is something we don't want our Chinese hosts to overhear, so we'll walk down that hallway a few steps and move into our sound-proof room. We call it 'the bubble,' it's made of clear plastic all around with a sound generator to mask anything that might escape - - -

"Okay. Where to begin? One important piece of this puzzle you don't yet know about because the Department approved the plan after you left the States.

"Oh?"

"Yes. There's a man on my staff that you've never heard of. Name is Gary Clark, his wife is Li Na Clark, before they were married her name was Li Na Lin, born and raised right here in Hubei province.

"Gary is our PPO, Publications Procurement Officer. He and Li Na both speak—and write—Mandarin. His job is to move around the province and collect open information: newspapers, magazines, propaganda fliers, whatever. When they study this stuff, carefully, even though it's all open material, they'll sometimes find a nugget or two of useful intelligence.

"And there's more. After some back and forth with the Department, we decided that your—our—project should include a *Christian* component. That's where Gary comes in. He's a born-again Christian, good friend of Franklin Graham, served on Graham's Samaritan's Purse Board of Directors. Much earlier, he was a friend of Bill Bright, attended Bright's Christian Executive seminar at Arrowhead Springs, part of Bill's very effective Campus Crusade for Christ movement."

"Excuse me, Dick, but what has this to do with our project?"

"Good question, Jeff. Although I'm not a believer myself, I can see where a Christian ambience could be a big help. Let's face it, most if not all, of these homeless people have never been inside a church, much less a Christian church.

Some of them may be vaguely aware of Confucius and his teachings, not that it would help them much. And as soon as the word gets around that Christianity is alive and well, here in Wuhan, we can expect other Christians to appear, We know there are many local citizens who listen to Christian radio broadcasts from KHCB Radio Network in Houston, Texas. The rulers in Beijing don't like it, but there's not much they can do about it."

———————————◆◆◆———————————

Applications for admittance to the new shelter were already part of Dick Albright's filing system. Each one provided a summary of the applicant's life history, along with a photograph. So far, he had six of them.

1. Li Min Wong, 18 year old mother with 2 year old daughter. Father unknown. She's addicted to heroin, lives in a car, begs for food for self and infant.

Her unlikely story follows:

———————————◆◆◆———————————

The authorities had decided to turn off the lights in the village's one park, claiming it was needed to reduce the strain on the area's electric grid. The timing could not have been worse because a cold, damp wind was blowing in off the sea, threatening to either move everything in its path or soak it beyond recognition. Li Min Wong was clutching her two year old daughter, the two of them crammed into the back seat of an abandoned vehicle, the only shelter within at least one kilometer. The vehicle's windows had been blown out and infant Li Na had soaked her diaper and was beginning to cry. Li Min reached into one of her pockets, found an almost dry cigarette, lighted it and began to feel better. The heroin-laced smoke always had this same effect; too bad her daughter was much too young to smoke. In another pocket she found the faux nipple she was looking for, placed in the infant's mouth and the infant soon quieted, sound asleep.

She guessed it was about five in the morning, still dark and stormy. At dawn's first light, Li Min would struggle to get out of the car, wrap her daughter in an overlarge shawl and walk the half-kilometer to Chi Wong's grocery. She had done this many times; Chi Wong was always willing to give her *something* to eat, and bottled formula for her daughter.

But it was not to be. Chi Wong had alerted one of the neighborhood foot patrolmen to be on the lookout for this 'vagrant female' and her daughter. As she was about to enter the grocery - - -

"Is that you, Li Min? Yeah, I thought so, same as yesterday and the day before. Well, I've got some good news. There's a shelter for homeless folks, like you and your daughter, not too far from here. You hop into my patrol car and I'll take you there, the baby, too. I understand it doesn't cost anything and you'll meet and make friends with others, like yourself."

"You sure it's free? Ain't got no money. And what about my baby? She's welcome?"

"She is. But if you decide to move into the shelter and stay there, you'll have to stay clean for at least three months. No more pot, no more booze. Can you do that?"

"I've tried and it's hard. But don't have much choice, do I? How do I apply?"

"You don't. I'll drive you there, take about fifteen minutes, and I'll introduce you to the folks who run the place."

"Better hurry, baby needs new diaper."

"Hey, Chen Bu, look down there. That's our friend sergeant Li Wei, and he has a woman and a baby with him, they're coming our way. Do you suppose - - -?"

"Could be, our very first homeless residents. I'm on my way, keep your fingers crossed!"

Chen Bu's first task was to assure this frightened woman that she was safe. She quickly found a diaper and asked the mother to change it. That done, she asked her new client to sit down. Yes, It's oaky to hold your child why we talk, but I need to know a lot more before we can help you.

Chen Bu knew that what might follow would be her first opportunity to talk to one of the region's many homeless people, and these were two.

"What's your name?"

"Li Min Wong."

"And your baby's?"

"No name, not yet."

"Are you married?"

"No. Don't remember who."

"How is that?"

"Had too much rice wine; he forced his thing into me. Make baby."

"You were *raped*?"

"Guess so."

"Does he know you're here?"

"Don't know."

"Okay, Li Min, you're welcome to stay here but there are a few things we need to know. For one, where were you born, and when?"

"Don't know."

"You're sure?"

"Daddy left when I was young. Mother said forget about him."

"You should have some kind identification, your government requires it."

"Maybe, but lost it."

"When you emptied you pockets you put things on this table. A cigarette and a nipple for your baby. Do you smoke?"

"Have to. Feel better."

"How is that?"

"Guy sells me stuff, put in cigarette. Feel better."

"Do you remember when you began doing this?"

"Long time ago."

"Have you ever tried to quit?"

"Many times, but very hard."

"Okay, Li Min. You're welcome to stay here, with your baby, but you *must* try to quit smoking. Other people live here and we don't want them to know that you're addicted. Do you know what means, *addicted.*?"

"No, but sounds bad."

"Yes, it is bad. But that's okay. Here's what you need to do. You go into that room over there. Leave your baby with me. After you close the door, you take all your clothes off and turn on the shower. There are two handles, one for hot and one for cold. When the water feels comfortable, you reach for a bar of soap and wash yourself, your hair, too. Then you dry yourself

53

with a towel and come back here. While you're doing that, I'm going to wash your baby, put a new diaper on her."

"She hungry, probably."

"What has she been eating?"

"No eat; formula."

"That's fine; we have a supply of formula right here."

"What's next?"

"We're going to give you a new set of clothes, we'll burn your old ones; same for your baby. Then, I'll take you to your apartment. It's new, has everything you need including a crib for your baby. Inside the apartment you'll find a list of things you should do.

"You do read, don't you?"

"Think so."

TEN

One week later - - -

"How's are new residents doing?"

"It's tough. Doctor Woo saw her yesterday, said it's typical for addicts to have these painful withdrawal symptoms. He gave me ten doses of Methadone, showed me how to use it—the tablets dissolve in water—and I'm to see to it that she drinks a full glass of water during her breakfast meal."

"Probably tastes awful."

"Yes, but he told me to add a half-teaspoon of sugar to the mix. I've tried that and she's getting used to it"

"How about the baby?"

"Thank God! She's doing just fine. I put a bundle of Pampers in her room, showed Li Min how to use them. She's taking the formula four times a day, bowels are fine and she's gaining weight"

"What about a name?"

"Yes, we talked about that. Li Min thinks her family, over the generations, has had a naming ceremony. Family members gather and the oldest—usually a grandfather or great-grandfather—recites a prayer (something handed down from Confucius, believe it or not), speaks the new name carefully so that everyone understands it, and that does it."

"Has she chosen a name?"

"Not yet, she said it's important and she wants to think about it."

"Well, when she *does* decide we can have our own naming ceremony. I'm sure she'll like that."

"Okay, Chen Bu, who's next on our list?"

"This is a tough one, Jeff. Her name is Wang Jing Tang, she's 48 and she recently owned and operated one of the city's more popular brothels. Doctor Woo told me she has syphilis and probably won't live more than another year, maybe two. He knows how to cure syphilis but it's a very long procedure, usually takes at least a year. So if we allow her to come here and live, we can be pretty sure she'll die here. And if that's not enough, her husband walked out on her when he learned of her illness.

"That means she was once a wealthy woman, aside from how she made her money, and now she's dirt poor.

"What do you think?"

"Chen Bu, let's not forget that this business of ours is supposed to have a *Christian* outlook. You'll recall that Jesus cured all kinds of people: the lame, a few with leprosy, even that blind beggar, Bartimaeus. I consider that a challenge, so, yes, we will allow this woman to come live with us. Her disease is not transferable, others who live near her cannot be infected. Actually, it's better if the others don't know about her illness. We'll treat her just like the others. We can ask Doctor Woo if she needs a special diet, but that won't be a problem."

"What about her customers, the men who made her wealthy? They're likely to find out where she is; they might even want to come visit her."

"Well, any man who can afford visits to a brothel is unlikely to be homeless. We'll allow him—them—to come for a visit but that's all."

"Okay, Jeff. Who's next?"

"Yeah, this should be interesting. His name is Li Jie Han; he's 50, used to operate a repair shop for bicycles and vacuum cleaners. He's never married, admits he's gay. When the shop's owner learned of this, he fired him, fearing he probably has AIDs."

"So if we agree to allow him to come here, we should ask doctor Woo to examine him. If he refuses the examination he doesn't come."

"That's what I would say."

———— ·◆· ————

Ten days later - - -

"Mr. Han, we've received you application but I have a few questions."

"Sure, go ahead."

"You'll recall your examination by Dr. Woo, three days ago?"

"Of course I remember. He told me I don't have AIDs."

"Did he say anything about your attraction to other men?"

"What's that supposed to mean?"

"Look, Mr. Han, there are any number of men in this

neighborhood, not to mention the few who work here. They'll soon learn that you're gay. How do you supposed they'll react, when they learn this?"

"How should I know? But, what's your point?"

"My point, Mr. Han, is this. IF we allow you take up residence here, we'll expect you to be celibate, for as long as you're here. Do you know what that means?"

"You mean no sex, right?"

"Yes."

"How about women?"

"That, too. That's what 'celibate' means. No sex, no how."

"Maybe I should cut it off."

"No need to be vulgar, Mr. Han. Do you want to live here or don't you?"

"Of course I do. You should know that."

"Okay. You can move in tomorrow but you need to behave yourself for at least the first month. If can't do that, you can stay where you are. Fair enough?"

"Got it."

ELEVEN

"This one is different, Sweetheart."

"Oh?"

"It's a letter from a high school teacher, he teaches chemistry and physics at Zen Li high school, about ten kilometers from here."

"And?- - -"

"Yeah, I got on the phone a half hour ago and asked to speak to the principal of the school. The teacher's name is Wang lei Zheng, he's 32 and his wife left him six weeks ago."

"Why'd she do that?"

"Seems he persuaded one of his female students to stay after school. She's 17 and quite attractive. They had a couple of glasses of wine, one thing led to another, and he winds up raping her, right there on his classroom floor. The girl's parents have threatened to sue the school, and they will if she's found to be pregnant."

"And he wants to come and live here?"

"The school's principal told me he/they understand that anyone is welcome, so long as he/she is homeless. And as soon as she left him, the wife contacted a real estate agent and the home is about to be sold. So, yes, he's homeless, or soon will be."

"But he'll have enough money to buy another home, won't he?"

"The principal told me the ex-wife has hired an attorney and the two of them intend to render the poor guy penniless. So, no. If he comes here, he won't have a dime."

"What will our other residents think, if they learn he's admitted to raping a young girl.?

"We'd want to assure him that our lips are sealed. And is lips are already sealed, most likely."

"Okay, you tell him we'll expect him to arrive within the week, and we'll go from there."

Wang lei Zheng arrived on time, Jeff was there to mee him. The two men sat down in Jeff's office. Chen Bu decided to let her husband do the talking.

"So, welcome to our modest office. Do I call you Wang Lei or Mr. Zheng?"

"I'd prefer the former, if it makes no difference to you."

"Good. I'd like you to tell me how you envision your stay here. What would you like to do?"

"Let's begin by talking, briefly, about my past and why I'm here. Yes, I made a huge mistake with that young student. I learned only yesterday that she's not pregnant and her parents don't intend to pursue the matter. As to what I'd like to do, I have an idea for you to consider."

"I'm listening."

"I understand that this homeless shelter, as you call it, was at one time a hotel. I assume this hotel has a lobby, perhaps even a conference room. Here's what I'm proposing.

"As you know, I am, or was, a high school teacher, physics and chemistry my specialty. I would be quite willing to teach those subjects, and English, too, to your residents and to anyone else who might be interested. These lessons would be free, no charge, unless the participants might wish to make a donation to your shelter. As you can see, I speak both Mandarin and English, which broadens the number of students who might be interested. I'm hoping you can see this as a win-win opportunity, as the saying goes."

"I like it, Wang Lei. I'm sure my wife will too, as soon as I tell her. What about publicity?"

"Yes. I have a laptop computer with a Windows 10 operating system. I know that Microsoft sometimes contracts with one of our Chinese companies so I may be using an entirely 'Made in China' system. I know of several print shops in this vicinity, so we could begin advertising whenever you say so."

<hr />

It *was* a win-win situation. At last report, Wang Lei's hotel/classroom hosted 35 students, both sexes, ranging in age from 23 to 50. And there is a waiting list of nearly 70 more. After a few weeks of haggling, the local Chinese authorities agreed to give Wang Lei's graduates full credit, to be applied to any further education they might pursue.

TWELVE

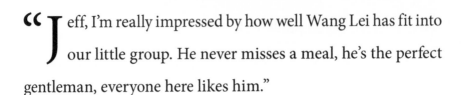

"Jeff, I'm really impressed by how well Wang Lei has fit into our little group. He never misses a meal, he's the perfect gentleman, everyone here likes him."

"You're right, Chen Bu. The other day I saw him with that little orphan kid who comes around here now and then. He's may be eight, not a day older, and Wang Lei is teaching him how to add and subtract, even multiply. He gave the child a cell phone and is teaching him how to use it."

"Yes, and word like this gets around. I know the director of that orphanage, where little Wang Lei lives and he believes a few of his friends may be dropping by. Perhaps we should buy a few more cell phones."

"Yes, we can do that. There's a shop just a few blocks from here that sells them. For American money, we can buy one for 35 dollars, and that's well within our budget.

"Okay, Jeff. Who's next?"

"We don't know much about this guy, only what the referral sheet tells us. Name is Wang Lei Fong. He's 38, a male nurse who's employment at a local hospital was terminated three weeks ago."

"Why terminated?"

"The hospital fired him when management learned that he'd been having sex with one of his patients, a 40 year old woman who was about to be released after recovering from a serious car accident. Killed her husband and two children. Wang Lei is divorced, has no children. His—our—problem is that he's addicted to crack cocaine. He apparently knows how to buy this stuff from a pusher who is working right here in our neighborhood."

"Hmm. We already have one addict. Accepting another shouldn't be so hard. What do you think?"

"We'll have to ask Doctor Woo about that."

———◆◆◆———

It was no surprise that Doctor Woo replied that having one more addict shouldn't matter. He reminded that he has plenty of Methadone and he knows how to prescribe it. But when Wang Lei sat down with Jeff for his interview, things did not go well.

"Welcome, Mr. Fong, we believe you'll like it here. It is your intention to join our group, is it not?"

"That depends."

"Depends on what?"

"You know damned well that I'm an addict. Otherwise I wouldn't come within three kilometers of this place. And I know something about Methadone, a few of my buddies have tried it. It hurts like hell at first and it takes weeks to get use to it. And if that's all you have to offer, I'm not sure I want to sign up. What say you?"

"It's really up to you. No one is forcing you to live here. You might want to talk to some of our residents, perhaps they could reassure you."

"How do I do that."

"Tell you what. You walk over there, to that conference room; that's part of our facility. You wait there five or ten minutes and you'll be able to chat with one of our residents, a young mother who, at one time, lived in a car with her infant daughter. Her name is Li Min Wong and as far as I know she's over her addiction and is doing quite well."

"Okay, I'll do that but I want you to be there, too."

The meeting lasted no more than fifteen minutes. Jeff was amazed at how the young woman's speech had improved. She had gained weight, her eyes had a certain sparkle and it took her no more than five minutes to persuade her would-be antagonist that he, too, could handle the Methadone treatment. That fact that Wang Lei Fong was old enough to be the young woman's father only added to his embarrassment. He reluctantly agreed to become a resident.

"Well, Jeff, I'd say we're doing pretty well. The few residents we have seem to like each other, at least there haven't been any fights. The two who are using Methadone are doing better, although they still have some time to go.

"Who's next on your list of applicants?"

"His name is Wang Yong Deng, and he's much different from the others."

"Oh?"

"Yes. He's only 28 and until recently, he was an athletic coach at that high school, about five kilometers from here."

"You say *was*."

"Yeah, he was fired by the high school principal for having sex with an 18 year old female gymnast. He's an accomplished guy, trained those kids in soccer, tennis and—his favorite— gymnastics. So far, no one knows the name of his girl friend; the sex was consensual, but the fact that she's also a student is what got him in trouble."

"Why does he want to come here?"

"Because he's admitted to the principal that his sex drive is so strong, he's afraid he might try it again, on someone else. He figures that by moving here, he can get over the urge. Has his victim complained?"

"No. Like I said, it was okay with her. If he comes here, she may want to visit him. Wouldn't that be a hoot!"

"Well, okay. Let's welcome him, with the understanding that he's on probation. Ninety days behaving himself or he leaves."

<hr />

The ninety days passed sooner than most expected. Wang Yong determined to be a model resident. He worked out regularly, jogged for twenty minutes each morning, did 50 pushups before breakfast.

Jeff and Chen Bu decided it was okay for him to invite his girlfriend for a visit and she turned out to be something very few expected. Wang Xiu Ying was a beautiful young woman. She excelled on the parallel bars, she even developed a modest dance routine, displaying her nimble profile. Within a few days, she was the most popular person in the neighborhood. Even though everyone knew that she was Wang Yong's paramour, it didn't seem to matter.

THIRTEEN

"Jeff, there's something we need to talk about, something I learned only a few hours ago."

"Sure, Chen Bu, what is it?"

"I was having a cup of tea with doctor Woo and he told me something that really concerns me.

"Yesterday afternoon, a young woman walked into his office. She introduced herself as Li Na Wong, she's 18 and had just escaped—her word—from a brothel, one located on the other side of the city. She claims to have been a sex slave and she used nearly the last of her earnings to pay for the taxi ride to Dr. Woo's office. The doctor asked her to disrobe, which she reluctantly did, and he examined her, looking for signs of venereal disease or anything else that might interfere with her eventual rehabilitation. After the exam, the two of them chatted for some time and he describes her as a beautiful young woman.

Her parents died when she was but twelve years old, some relatives took her in and with their help she began taking voice lessons. Now, he says, she has a beautiful soprano voice and could probably catch on with a professional group of musicians, say a small dance band or something like that.

"That's the good news. The bad news is that she's broke, and has no place to live. And the good doctor is hoping she could come here."

"I don't see why not. She sounds like the kind of person we should welcome."

———————◆◆———————

Welcome, indeed. Within three weeks of her arrival, Li Na was using her laptop to pipe in the latest hit songs and she was giving dancing lessons to any of the residents brave enough to try. Word spread throughout the neighborhood and within days a talent scout appeared. He offered her a contract: 66,000 Yuan ($100) per hour for five musicians: a pianist, trombone, saxophone, drums and clarinet. $500 per hour for three hours of dance music, or $1,500 US.

With the owner's permission, the hotel lobby was converted

to a dance floor. Advertising flyers went out, inviting anyone to appear at 7 p.m. each Saturday evening. Come as you are.

"What do you think, Sweetheart? The local authorities will hear about this as soon as we open. Then what? We'll have to pay taxes?"

"No, Chen Bu. This will be a legal business arrangement, part of the United States Consulate General's budget. The Chinese cannot tax such an enterprise; it's written in our contract with the Chinese.

"Our problem is going to be how we limited the number of people who show up each Saturday evening, With the orchestra in place, there's room for what?--- maybe 30 couples?" We can charge each of them, say, the equivalent of ten U.S. dollars. We won't make any money but enough to pay the musicians."

"What about a name?"

"Yeah, I asked Li Na about that. She suggested we call it *Li Na's Paradise.* She's popular enough to get away with something like that. And she told me she's contacted one of the local newspapers for publicity and she wants to set up her own Web page."

"Can she do that on her own or does she need government permission?

"She's already hired a lawyer, believe it or not. And he tells her to go ahead. If the authorities object, he'll take care of it."

"And you have one more name on your list, someone who might want to come here?"

"Yes, I do. His name is Zhang Yong Win, he's 20 years old, good looking guy. He's been painting houses throughout the neighborhood but has had to quit. The fumes have made him so dizzy he can't continue working. He told me he saved enough money to go to a doctor and the doctor insisted that he quit and look for a safe place to live. He'll be here first thing tomorrow morning."

———◆◆◆———

A romance made in Heaven? Maybe not, but within a month after moving into the homeless shelter, Zhang Yong and Li Na announced their intention to marry. After several dates, Li Na learned that, in addition to paining houses, Zhang Yong plays the bass fiddle about as well as anyone can. So he's now part of her orchestra which continues to draw as many young people as the dance floor can accommodate. And they're making money, too, all of it going to support the shelter.

FOURTEEN

Wang Wei Fong's trial was as good as over. Wuhan's largest brokerage firm had produced not one, but three witnesses who, under oath, told the jury that Wang Wei had defrauded ten of his company's clients to the tune of some 50 million Yuan, the equivalent of nearly ten million American dollars.

Faced with this evidence he decided—against the advice of his lawyer—to plead guilty and let the judge determine his fate.

Judge Lei: "Mr. Fong, this court wants to be fair about this but in view of the gravity of your crime I'm inclined to send you to prison. What say you?"

"Judge, please don't do that. I'm 65 years old. My wife has left me and I never see my kids and grandkids. They're treating me like a criminal and I can't say I blame them. Worse, I have no place to go because my wife has already sold our home. I guess that makes me 'homeless.'

"Yes it does, Mr. Fong. And I happen to know of a shelter for homeless people. I would urge you to apply for admittance. If you do that, I'll change my mind about prison."

"Thank you, judge. Thank you very much."

"So, Jeff, do we admit this man? A 65 year old swindler?"

"It would be a first, Chen Bu. But we've never turned down anyone up to now. So I say yes, let's welcome him."

And welcome him they did. Wang Wei Fong has his own room, on the second floor, with all the amenities one could wish. However, his experience in the court room, with so many of his peers present—and laughing behind his back—has made him a nervous wreck. So that now he's developed a dependency on crack cocaine.

"Jeff, Wang Wei came down for dinner yesterday and he was

barely able to walk, 'stoned,' as they say. We should insist that he spend some time with doctor Woo."

"I agree, Chen Bu, and I'll tell him that. Either he kicks his habit or he's back on the streets. They call this *Tough Love,* I believe."

———————◆◆◆———————

Physicians and knowledgeable lay people know that—even with the help of Methadone—withdrawal symptoms can be so painful that the infected person wishes he/she were dead. But after six months of unimaginable suffering, Wang Wei Fong has righted himself and now is a welcome member his small community.

———————◆◆◆———————

"Jeff, this applicant, from what I see on paper, breaks my heart."

"How so, Sweetheart?"

"Her name is Zhang Li Wan, she's 75 years old and she has Parkinson's disease. And everyone knows that disease is fatal, there's no cure for it. Her application also tells us that she's a widow and that her kids and grandkids never come to see her; they're afraid they'll catch what she has."

"Hmm. About all doctor Woo can do is prescribe Levodopa. That drug is not a cure but it's supposed to ease the patient's symptoms; less pain, fewer stumbles. We do have a walker, don't we."

"Yes, we do. No one here has had a need for it, but Mrs. Wan surely will."

Weeks later, Jeff's diary recorded an unhappy ending. Zhang Lie Wan somehow obtained access to a .38 revolver, put it her mouth and pulled the trigger.

———————◆◆◆———————

"Jeff, you and I knew that, sooner or later, we'd have to stop accepting new applicants. For two months now, with the exception of what happened to Zhang Lie Wan, this operation has been running like a Swiss watch, hard to believe but it's true. There's an old saying, 'Maybe We Should Quit While We're Ahead.' Do you think it's time?"

"Yes, I do, Sweetheart. However, there's one thing we have

not yet accomplished and I know you're thinking the same thing."

"The CG's new hire, Gary Clark?"

"That's the one. His wife, Li Na, before they were married, was Li Na Min. Gary is the consulate's PPO, Publications Procurement Officer. Both of these young people speak excellent Mandarin. Gary's job requires that he move around the Hubei province as much he can—he has his own automobile, a well-worn Toyota Prius—to collect newspapers, magazines, pamphlets, brochures, anything and everything that tells readers what is *really* going on throughout the province, especially how the average Chinese citizen is dealing with the Coronavirus and Covid-19. And, of course, he reports all this, through the CG, to the State Department in Washington. And Li Na usually goes with him. She's a very attractive young woman and people enjoy talking to her."

"But that's not all, is it?"

"No, certainly not. Gary and his wife are born-again Christians. Gary was, at one time, on the board of directors of Franklin Graham's Samaritan's Purse ministry. They both knew

Bill Bright, before he died, and they attended one of Bright's Christian Executive seminars in Arrowhead Springs, California.

"Gary has the CG's blessing to speak to our group. Two days ago he asked me to give each of our residents a Bible, written in Mandarin, a long-ago project by some Campus

Crusade for Christ volunteers. I've told him we've set up a bunch of chairs on the floor of the hotel lobby, there's an adequate PA system and he's ready.

For Gary and his wife, this was something they'd practiced many times. Audience participation is the key, get you listeners thinking about how *they* feel about what you're about to say (first question: who was Jesus of Nazareth?)

"Li Jie Han, what do you remember reading about Jesus of Nazareth?"

"Well from what I read yesterday, I don't believe a word of it. Said he was crucified, dead and buried and on the third day he rose and went to heaven, to be with God."

"Li Min, what about you?"

"I read the story about how Jesus turned water into wine. Whoever wrote that must have been smoking something. How could anyone do that?"

"Wang Yong, it's your turn."

"Yeah, that story about Jesus walking on water seems to me to be just a legend. If I tried to walk on water I'd be dead in three minutes!"

"Good. It's pretty clear that each of you is skeptical about what you've read. And that's not unusual. Thousands, maybe millions, of readers react the same way. So let's break this down into parts that make sense.

"For one, we can identify the people who knew Jesus, personally. That would include Matthew, the author of the first gospel; John, the writer of the fourth gospel, Peter, probably the man closest to Jesus and James, Jesus' half-brother.

"Luke, as you should know, never knew Jesus. He was an historian and a very good one."

"We're not sure about Mark, but the experts believe that he got most of his information from his friend, Peter.

"Then, there's Paul. Paul comes along after Jesus' death and resurrection. You read his account of what happened to him on the road to Damascus. He was miraculously changed to be a strong advocate for the truth about Jesus. And, his writings count for most of the New Testament texts.

"Wang Jing, you wanted to say something?"

"I sure do. What if all this is a lot of fairy tales, a bunch of old men in black robes sit down and make it up, then get rich preaching a lie. What does that give us!??"

"Fair enough, Wang Jing. I'll try to explain.

"We've identified Matthew, John, Peter and James as men who knew Jesus, personally. Then there's Luke and Mark and, last but not least, Paul. That's seven different men, each of them telling the same story or similar stories.

"So here's the question each of you should think about, very carefully:

"Why would each of these seven men write these stories, knowing for sure that the Romans would read them, and then, almost certainty, put them to death for claiming a King other than Caesar? Maybe one or two, but *all seven*???

"Think about it, use your common sense!

"Wang Yong, your hand is raised."

"Sure is. You haven't yet said a word about God. The Bible claims that in the beginning he made the heavens and earth. I understand that Moses is the author of this claim but what if Moses is wrong, or that he made it up just to sound important to his friends?"

"Okay, here's part of my answer. Have you looked up at the stars lately, after it's real dark?"

"Sure I have. Everybody does that."

"Ask yourself this: how did those stars get there?"

"Probably nobody knows."

"Another idea. We all know there are nine planets in our solar system, one of them being our planet earth. They rotate around the sun, takes earth 365 days to do this. How much does the earth weigh? I looked it up on Google and the number is 1024 *tons*. That's multiplying ten by itself 24 times. That number is so huge it's impossible to imagine it. So here's the question: What keeps an object so huge in an orbit that never changes? My answer is *God*.

"Here's another idea. Everything out there, including the sun, the zillion stars and our earth and everything on it, is called *creation*. I think we can all agree on that. But for 'creation' to exist, there has to be a *creator.* And that creator is God. Who/what else could it be?

"Or, when you look at the ocean or a very large lake, how do those get there? Or when a baby is born and she resembles her mother. How does this happen?

"How should I know?"

"Wang Yong, we're talking about miracles, and miracles *do* happen. But they happen only because God allows them to happen."

"Hmm. Well, I admit I never thought about it that way. Maybe you're right."

———◆◆◆———

Gary noticed a few smiles and nodding heads. He promised to be back tomorrow.

FIFTEEN

"Okay, Li Na, it's time to go. I doubt there are any charging stations along our route and even if there were, our beat-up Prius would prefer gasoline. What's our first stop?"

"Gary, why don't we walk over to that newsstand? That vendor has newspapers from all over the province and he talks to a lot of people. You can use your digital voice recorder, tell him you want to record whatever he has to say so that you won't make any mistakes. If he asks why, you tell him the truth, that you're writing articles for American readers, people who are anxious to learn what's happening here in Hubei province. Everybody knows this is where the Coronavirus got its start, right here in that lab."

"Good idea, Li Na."

Gary's report, first to appear in The San Francisco Examiner *and read by most of China Town's residents, in both English and Mandarin.*

"According to well-informed sources here in Hubei province, the Covid-19 epidemic continues its rampage, especially in those rural regions where health care facilities are far and few between. One report, provided by a physician who claims to know, says that as many as 75 to 100 of his patients die each week. The nearest morgue has refused to accept more bodies, many of which are taken directly to cemeteries where they are buried, usually without the knowledge of next of kin.

"Aside from the human pain and suffering, most citizens are furious at their government's refusal to accept responsibility for what is happening. Chairman Xi's propagandists continue to insist that the Chinese government is doing everything humanly possible to thwart the spread of the disease, when the look-around evidence says otherwise.

"One example—one of many—illuminates the truth. Eight year old Li Jing Woo was orphaned when she was but five years old. The orphanage that took her in now cares for about fifty children, most under the age of twelve. Because the orphanage lies in a rural area, some 70 kilometers from the nearest city, it has yet to receive its first shipment of the anti-covid vaccine. The facility's manager, Li Jie Fong, predicts that as many as one-half of his young residents will die within the month, barring some kind of miracle."

———————◆———————

"That's a good beginning, Sweetheart, but lets move on. There's a village about 40 kilometers from here, has a small public park, and we'll find residents sitting on benches, especially with this lovely weather we've been having."

———————◆———————

Another report, again to appear in The San Francisco Examiner *and read by most of China Town's residents, in both English and Mandarin.*

"Most everyone knows that life in the city and life in the country are two different things. My wife and I dropped by a public park in the village of Na Wang, about 40 kilometers from our home. We found 35 year old Li Jun Fong, sitting on one of the park's benches.

"Li Jun works as a welder in a local machine shop, fabricating metal parts for a chain of hardware stores. I should say he *did* work. He was fired four days ago because he failed to bring to work that little certificate that say's he's received his second vaccination. His boss accused him of trying sabotage the shop by spreading the virus to his co-workers. Li Jun says that he's had enough experience and is good enough at what he does to set up his own welding shop. And he has several friends who will become part of his business. He'll need a start-up loan from a bank but he's sure that won't be a problem. He told us that if this were happening in a city, and not in a tiny village, the Chinese Communist authorities would find a way to either fine him or lay some kind of heavy tax on his business. And just before we left him, he wanted to know what it would be like to operate his business in the United States."

<hr>

"We found another bench-sitter in this same park. Her name is Li Jing Yang, she's 22, quite pretty but it was obvious that she'd been crying. Seems her boyfriend walked out on her earlier today. We told her she could share her sorrow and we'd keep it all to ourselves. This is what she told us.

"Her boy friend, Wang Wei Zan, is a 21 year old college dropout. He fancies himself as the most desirable man on Planet Earth, he jogs for an hour every morning, was on the school's track team before he quit. And he wants to have sex with Li Jing, at least three times a week.

"Of course she wants none of this but he's threatened to beat her up if she refuses. She's complained to one of the cops who strolls through the park every now and then but he says he can't do anything but sympathize with her. When she told the officer that she's certain Wang Wei has AIDs, he suggested she try to get him to go to the nearest hospital to seek treatment.

"She ended her story with a heavy sigh, reminding us that, in her opinion, in this workers' paradise, the Chinese Communist government, by choice, has no interest whatsoever in the affairs of its citizens."

SIXTEEN

*O*800 hours, Ft. Mead, Maryland, in the office of NSA's chief forecaster, Robert Heywood.

"Hey Joey, have a look at this latest satellite image."

"Yeah, Bob, I just saw it. A huge anticyclone over the Western Pacific. Winds already at 90 knots and likely to increase to 110 within the next six hours. That's hurricane strength and we're obliged to let the world know about it."

"Looks like the west coast of China will bear the brunt of this monster. There are probably a zillion Americans over there, tourists, business people, diplomats, a few military guys. Tell you what, let's alert the State Department first. Our embassy in Beijing will know where most of the Americans are and what they're doing. With enough warning time they can hunker down and ride out the storm."

"Okay, Joey. You send a cablegram to our embassy in Beijing, make it FLASH priority, they'll have it within a few minutes. Then we tell the White House, the Pentagon and the US Navy. They have ships standing off the Chinese coast, maybe they'll have time to seek refuge in one of the harbors."

———◆———

Franklin Hatfield, the U.S. ambassador to Beijing, was the first official to see the FLASH advisory, moments after it arrived from the embassy's message center. He phoned his communications officer.

"Harry, this is Franklin. It seems pretty obvious that as far inland as we are, that storm won't arrive for another twelve hours. But I'm worried about our other people, who know nothing about this. We have five consulates general out there. Please, asap, repeat this message to each one of them."

Ten minutes later Richard Albright had read the same message.

"Marie, this is bad news. There are least 200 American citizens scattered throughout Hubei province. We'll have to rely on Chinese radio broadcasts to let them know. We can however, and we will, get the word to everyone right here in Wuhan. We can begin with Jeff Winslow's homeless shelter. God only knows how much wind that building can withstand and Jeff and Chen Bu may wish to evacuate their residents. The safest place would the basement in this building. It has lights, hot and cold water, two shower stalls and a few toilets. Please tell Jeff, now."

EPILOGUE

As it happened, the storm inflicted minimal damage to the city and most of Hubei province. The shelter's residents were able to seek protection in the building's basement. Forty eight hours later, they reassembled in the shelter and life goes on.

In a quiet ceremony in the United States embassy in Beijing, ambassador Franklin Hatfield—on instructions from the State Department in Washington—awarded Jeff Winslow and his wife the Distinguished Service medal, in recognition of their exemplary service. The couple will be eligible for home leave in one more year.

ABOUT THE AUTHOR

John Sager is a retired United States intelligence officer whose services for the CIA, in various capacities, spanned more than a half-century. A widower, he makes his home in the Covenant Shores retirement community on Mercer Island, Washington.

©Yuen Lui Studio, 2003